A GIFT FOR:

_____

FROM:

_____

what are little girls made of?

sugar
and spice
and
everything...

fun

If you really want to
be happy, nobody
can stop you.

—Sister Mary Tricky

You will do
foolish things,
but do them with
enthusiasm.
—Colette

and

playful...

and
thoughtful

'Twas her thinking
of others made
you think of her.

—Elizabeth Barrett Browning

It takes each of us
to make a difference
for all of us.
—Jackie Mutcheson

and

caring...

and
vibrant

Let nothing dim the light
that shines from within.

—Maya Angelou

How we spend
our days, of course,
is how we spend
our lives.
—Annie Dillard

and

alive...

and
strong

Be afraid of nothing.
You have within you
all wisdom, all strength,
all understanding.

—Eileen Caddy

May troubles
leave you thick-
skinned but
tender inside.

—Marge Piercy

and
tender…

and
intelligent

Brilliance is one
part talent, two
parts wisdom and
three parts passion.

—Margaret Mitchell

Inspiration does
not come like a bolt,
it comes to us quietly
and all the time.

—Brenda Ueland

and

creative…

and
spontaneous

The soul should always
stand ajar, ready to welcome
the ecstatic experience.

—Emily Dickinson

You are unique,
and if that is
not fulfilled,
then something
wonderful
has been lost.

—Martha Graham

and

natural...

and
confident

Doubt who you will,
but never yourself.

—Christine Bovee

and

daring...

Take the leap,
and the net
will appear.

—Julie Cameron

and

magical

Love is the touch that transforms.

—Mildred Davis

Truth is beauty,
and beauty is truth.

—Simone Bedford

and
real…

and

honest...

Who I am is more important
than where I'm going.
—Francoise Arnoux

I am not afraid.
I was born
to do this.

—Joan of Arc

and
heroic

and
curious

Where there is an open mind,
there will always be a frontier.

—Dorothea Brande

Be strong, go with
your heart, and
believe in miracles
because anything,
anything can happen.

—Marlo Javidando

and
faithful...

and
resourceful

I don't believe in luck.
We make our own
good fortune.

—Dr. Joyce Brothers

Creative minds have always been known to survive any kind of bad training.

—Anna Freud

and
resilient...

and

passionate

There is only one big
thing—desire—and
when it is big, all is little.

—Willa Cather

What we have once enjoyed we can never lose. All that we love deeply becomes a part of us.

—Helen Keller

and loving...

and

positive

It's so hard when I have to,
and so easy when I want to.

—Sondra Anice Barnes

Life is fragrant with possibilities.
—Kelly Ann Rothaus

and aspiring...

and all
things good
in the
world...

that's what
little girls
are
made of.

Designed by Steve Potter
Compiled by Dan Zadra & Kobi Yamada

COM·PEN·DI·UM™
Publishing

$\mathcal{E}$nriching the lives of millions, one person at a time.™

This book may be ordered directly from the publisher, but please try your
local bookstore first! To see Compendium's full line of inspiring products
visit us at www.compendiuminc.com or call toll free 800-91-IDEAS.

ISBN: 1-932319-07-7

Printed in China